Original title:
Growing Grace

Copyright © 2025 Creative Arts Management OÜ
All rights reserved.

Author: Vivienne Beaumont
ISBN HARDBACK: 978-1-80567-045-2
ISBN PAPERBACK: 978-1-80567-125-1

Hues of the Heart

In a world of colors bright,
I painted my dreams with delight.
One day I chose a shade of glee,
But ended up with broccoli!

Navigating the Unknown

I set sail on a sea of doubt,
With a map that was upside down.
The wind blew firmly in my hair,
I found a sandwich, but no fare!

Whispers of Transformation

The caterpillar reads self-help,
As it dreams of becoming a kelp.
It wiggles and wiggles, so afraid,
    Only to find it's a parade!

Ascending to the Light

I'm climbing high, so filled with hope,
On a rope that's just some soap.
With each slip and slide, I yell out loud,
"Mom, I swear I'll make you proud!"

Raindrops of Renewal

Puddles dance, and I slip and slide,
Rain's my partner, can't hide my pride.
Colors bloom, a hat on my head,
Bouncing like a frog, all thoughts of dread.

Socks are soaked, but I laugh out loud,
Twirling circles, feeling quite proud.
Umbrellas up, we twirl them 'round,
In puddles of joy, true bliss is found.

The Elixir of Time

Sipping tea with a twist of lime,
Every sip a tick, as I climb.
A clock that jokes as it spins, oh dear,
Time is a prankster, that much is clear!

Late for a meeting? Who could predict?
The cat steals the chair, what a neat trick!
I can't sit still, my thoughts go rogue,
In the circus of life, I juggle and vogue.

Melodies of the Heart

My heart sings tunes like a goofball's show,
With each thump, a new dance, on with the flow.
Shuffle my feet to the beat of the day,
Laughter's the rhythm that leads me, hooray!

Fumbling my steps, but hey, I smile wide,
Waltzing through failures, I'm taking the ride.
With friends by my side, it's a joyful spree,
We're a comical band, just let us be free.

Phoenix Ascending

From ashes I rise with a goofy grin,
Flames that tickle, let the fun begin!
Wings all aflutter, like feathers in flight,
I laugh with the fire, it tickles my sight.

Over the mountains, I'm soaring with flair,
My tail's on fire, but I have no care.
Like toast in the morning, I pop up anew,
Life's a breakfast buffet, and I'm ready for you!

From Burden to Blossom

I once was a weighty potato,
With worries that grew like a burrito.
But sprouted some leaves,
And danced with the breeze.

Now I'm a flower named Cheeto,
Poking fun at my old heavy veto.
I wiggle and swirl,
With colors that twirl.

Who knew spuds could be such a delight?
Unloading my baggage, I took flight.
Now I'm up high,
Where worries can't fry.

So if you feel stuck like a lump,
Just summon your strength and jump!
You might find a seed,
In the joy you can plead.

The Symphony of Growth

A seed in the dirt had a dream,
To join in a grand leafy theme.
But first came the rain,
Which felt like a pain.

It struggled and trembled a bit,
Worried it wouldn't make it fit.
But soon it could sing,
And dance in the spring.

Now it plays notes with the bees,
In a harmony tickling the trees.
A concert of joy,
Not a single downer to annoy.

So grab your gear and start the show,
Even roots have a rhythm to flow.
The garden's a stage,
For all at any age.

Phoenix from Ashes

I was a charred piece of toast,
As fiery as things could boast.
Then came a gust,
Turned my ash to dust.

Out popped a bird, bright and bold,
Talking like a jester of old.
With wings made of swag,
And a magical rag.

It soared through the sky with a cheer,
Shaking off traces of fear.
"From ashes I fly,
And I'll never say die!"

So if life scrambles you silly,
Just think of the bird, oh so frilly.
Rise up with a laugh,
And enjoy the sweet path.

Embers of Change

In the fireplace, I saw a spark,
Dancing around like a lark.
A smoldering glow,
That said, "Hey, let's go!"

With poking and prodding, I cheered,
Out came the flames, previously feared.
They flickered and flashed,
And suddenly splashed.

The embers became quite the party,
With marshmallows making things hearty.
All we needed was fun,
As the snacking begun!

So when life dares to toss a log,
Don't shy away, just dance like a frog.
Embrace every spark,
And light up the dark.

Woven in Time

In the garden of giggles,
Time weaves threads of cheer.
We tie our shoes together,
While chasing after deer.

Socks don't match, oh my!
But who really keeps score?
Laughter blooms like daisies,
As we tumble on the floor.

The clocks are all confused,
They tick-tock upside down.
We dance like silly puppets,
In this delightful town.

With every laugh that echoes,
Life's a comical rhyme.
In the fabric of our days,
We're woven through with time.

Unfolding the Spirit

Butterflies in pajamas,
Flap around in a haze.
We flip-flop with the sunshine,
And count our silly rays.

A cat that wears a hat,
Thinks she's the queen of cool.
With every purr and whisker,
She commands the whole school.

Every giggle is treasure,
As we bounce like a ball.
The spirit of fun dances,
In the midst of it all.

Each day's a new adventure,
With mischief in the air.
Unfolding all our laughter,
As we swirl without a care.

Cultivating Joy

Gardening with rubber boots,
We dig with laughter loud.
Pulling weeds of worry out,
Feeling funny and proud.

Flowers giggle in the breeze,
As we sing off-key tunes.
We water thoughts of happiness,
Beneath the chuckling moons.

With each sprout of joyful glee,
We jump and spin around.
Cultivating all the smiles,
Planted deep in the ground.

In this patch of silly bliss,
We harvest with such joy.
Each moment is a treasure,
For every girl and boy.

The Veil of Spring

Spring arrives like a puppy,
Wagging its tail with glee.
It rolls through all the meadows,
And plays tag with the bee.

Buds burst into laughter,
Colors wink and tease back.
Every bloom a giggle,
On the nature's fun track.

Daffodils don funny hats,
While the sun gives a grin.
We dance upon the meadows,
Letting all the fun in.

In the veil of playful days,
Joy's a whimsical fling.
As we frolic through the fields,
We can't help but sing.

Embracing Change

I woke up today with a strange new sock,
Turns out it was my pet's version of a rock!
Twirling around in mismatched shoes,
Life's a puzzle — with very odd clues.

When change creeps in, it's a wild surprise,
Like discovering a cake with no goodbyes!
I wear my wig like a crown of jest,
In this circus of life, I'll be the best!

Petals in the Wind

A daisy danced past with a wink and a spin,
It asked for a hand, but who'd let it win?
With petals like feathers, it giggled with glee,
Nature's confetti, so wild and so free.

It tumbled and fumbled right into my tea,
I laughed as it floated, just looking at me.
"Let's throw a party!" the flower declared,
But swatted by bees, it was hardly prepared!

Roots of Understanding

Deep down below, where the roots like to play,
They gossip and giggle in a muddy café.
"Did you hear what the tree said about the rain?"
"Don't ask! Last time, it went straight to its grain!"

The roots all chuckled, sharing secrets and tales,
While dodging the roots that told tricky old scales.
Together they grew with a giggling sway,
Turning each twist into fun, night or day.

Light Through Shadows

In the depths of the dark, a flashlight did slip,
It started a dance, with a flick and a flip.
Shadows were startled, took cover in fright,
As beams of pure laughter flooded the night.

"Why so gloomy?" the glow gently mused,
"Join in the fun! Don't sit there confused!"
So shadows shaped creatures with silly round eyes,
While laughter pulsed forth, lighting up the skies.

Echoes of Transformation

In the mirror, I see a clown,
With hair like a tornado, spinning round.
I thought I'd bloom into a flower,
Instead, I sprouted a funny power.

Chasing dreams on a rubber chicken,
My ambitions are as wild as a kitten.
With wiggles and giggles, I'll sway and twirl,
Transforming daily in this quirky whirl.

Seeds of Hope

I planted seeds in a shoebox tin,
Hoping for daisies but got a grin.
They sprouted socks, two left and one right,
Now I have a garden of mismatched delight!

Sunshine and rain keep knocking on my door,
To help my laughter burst and roar.
I water my hopes with lemonade,
And watch my silly blossoms invade!

Flourishing in Adversity

When life gives lemons, I make a pie,
With a dash of slapstick and silly spry.
Falling down is my favorite stunt,
I tumble and roll – it's a comedy hunt!

Embracing chaos, I dance on my face,
Each trip a twirl in this wacky race.
With every stumble, I find my stride,
Flourishing boldly in this joyride.

The Journey of the Soul

I packed my soul in a polka-dot bag,
A journey so silly it could make you lag.
With a map drawn in crayon, I set out to roam,
Adventuring big with my friend, the foam!

We hitch a ride on a unicycle,
Swapping tales and laughter while we recycle.
Each twist and turn brings rip-roaring laughs,
Growing wisely through all the silly gaffes!

A Garden of Dreams

In the plot where daisies dance,
I planted hopes, took a chance.
The weeds laughed loud, thought they were great,
But my flowers grew, it's never too late.

Sunflowers tall, a comical sight,
They bend and bow, in their delight.
A worm in a hat, with shades on tight,
Said, 'Life's a garden, grow what feels right!'

The carrots giggle beneath the dirt,
'Cause they're shy, and that's their quirk.
Bees buzz jokes, and butterflies cheer,
In this crazy garden, everyone's here!

So plant your laughter, rich and deep,
And watch as silly secrets creep.
Nature's chaos, a vibrant scheme,
In a garden that nurtures every dream.

Cradling the Future

In a cradle made of fallen leaves,
I nap with dreams as pure as thieves.
Squirrels prance, they steal my snacks,
But future plans stay on the tracks.

Clouds do cartwheels in the sky,
While raindrops giggle, oh my, oh my!
An acorn whispered, 'Don't be shy,
You'll be a tree, now don't you cry!'

The fish in puddles wear tiny hats,
And chirping frogs play tunes like bats.
Each hop they take, a joyful leap,
In this cradle where we sow and reap.

So hold onto hope, and don't lose track,
In this funny journey, there's no going back.
With laughter and love, we'll forge the path,
Cradling dreams with a goofy laugh.

Illuminated Pathways

Beneath the moon, the raccoons chat,
'Let's dance with shadows, how about that?'
Streetlights giggle, flickering bright,
Leading the way through the whimsical night.

Worms in bowties strut with flair,
They wiggled and jiggled, without a care.
A path of sparkles, oh what a sight,
Where laughter glimmers, pure delight!

The owls are wise, but they love to tease,
'Whooo's got jokes? Come on, if you please!'
Every turn a chuckle, every step a grin,
In this illuminated world, where fun begins.

So take a stroll, embrace the fun,
With every step, you're never done.
The pathways whisper, playful and free,
In a night filled with joy, just you and me.

The Colors of Change

In autumn's palette, leaves do a jig,
Twisting and turning, the colors so big.
Pumpkins smile wide, they're happy and round,
With faces that laugh without making a sound.

Spring brings giggles, the blooms start to sway,
Flowers in tutus, they dance and play.
A clumsy bee trips, falls on his face,
But gets up quick, 'What a silly place!'

Summer's a splash, a vibrant array,
The sun wears shades, taking a ray.
Kids with ice cream all over their clothes,
In the garden of laughter, everybody knows!

And winter's here with its frosty cheer,
Snowflakes twirl, 'Oh, do stick around here!'
Through all these colors, we'll endlessly roam,
Finding joy in each moment, forever at home.

Climbing New Heights

I tried to climb a tall tree today,
My pants got stuck—oh, what a display!
With squirrels laughing, I hung in mid-air,
Guess my height dreams can wait; it's not fair.

My friends cheered on with popcorn and drinks,
But all I could do was sit back and think.
Maybe next time I'll bring a good rope,
Or just stick to the ground—it's safer, I hope!

In the Arms of Growth

Tangled in vines while seeking some peace,
I thought I'd find calm but just found a fleece.
A bear passed by—he seemed quite confused,
I waved with a grin, he looked mildly amused.

I tried yoga beneath a big blooming plant,
The petals fell down—now my socks look quite scant.
Namaste, dear roots, let's sway in the breeze,
Just keep your branches away from my knees!

The Seedling's Journey

As a seed, I dreamed of being so tall,
But my sprout's more like a lopsided sprawl.
Twirling with wind, my leaves dance a jig,
Who knew that was all? I feel like a twig.

Nutrients come in—my stomach's a mess,
Though sunlight is great, I still feel the stress.
With worms as my buddies, we share all our woes,
They dig up my roots, but hey—everyone grows!

Authentic Awakening

Woke up one day with my roots all askew,
Looked in the mirror and said, "Who are you?"
My petals are ruffled, my stem's in a twist,
I laughed at my state—oh, who could resist?

I tried a new look, added some bright blooms,
Swapped leafy attire for frilly costumes.
A butterfly stopped, said, "Work it, my friend!"
I twirled with glee, hoping this style won't end!

Threads of Serenity

In a world of tangled thread,
My cat sits on my head.
She purrs like a fuzzy ball,
Life seems silly after all.

With a stitch and a snip,
I craft my own trip.
Each knot is a dance,
In life's bright romance.

A quilt of odd patches,
Where laughter matches,
Each color, a quirk,
Just a little smirk!

So here's to the seams,
That burst with our dreams.
In chaos, we find,
A joy that's aligned.

Harmony in Bloom

Flowers talk back in spring,
They yell, 'Oh, what a fling!'
Bees buzz in a dance,
Are they chasing romance?

The sun gives a wink
To the flowers that think.
'You're quite a sight,' he beams,
As they share wacky dreams.

Then comes the rain,
Bringing octopus pain,
With roots all in knots,
They giggle a lot!

In this botanical chatter,
Nothing else seems to matter.
The petals all sway,
As they jump into play.

The Tapestry of Life

We weave with yarns of the past,
Some colors bright, some aghast.
Oops, there goes a stitch,
Life can be quite a glitch!

Grandma's patterns, a delight,
Yet some threads just don't fight,
A pattern of laughter,
With chaos thereafter.

Each patch tells its tale,
Of the times we set sail.
With frays and all that jazz,
We dance with the pizazz!

So let's tug at those threads,
Forget about our beds.
In this fabric of cheer,
We stitch on without fear.

Perennial Promises

Promises sprout like weeds,
With giggles, we plant our seeds.
Some grow tall, some just flop,
Yet all make us laugh and stop.

In the garden of jest,
We dig up the best,
Each flower is quirky,
A little bit jerky.

With a wink to the sky,
We ask for a pie,
The fruit trees agree,
Let's bake it with glee!

May our hearts be aglow,
With a comical show.
Tendrils of fun spread wide,
In this wild, silly ride.

Creating New Horizons

In a garden of dreams that we planted wide,
We found some lost socks and a flower inside.
Spinning in circles, our smiles began,
Chasing our shadows, oh yes, we ran!

With paint on our fingers, we splashed the sky,
Who knew that clouds could giggle and fly?
Frolicking fields of bright polka dot,
Mixing our colors in a big, happy pot!

The sun wore sunglasses, looking quite fab,
And daisies danced grateful for all that they nab.
We're explorers of fun, through the fields we bounce,
Counting the chuckles, oh, so we pounce!

In this canvas of laughter, we twirl and glide,
Creating new horizons, with dreams as our ride!

The Spiral of Life

Round and round, we spin without care,
Like spaghetti on forks, we twirl in the air.
Each twist and turn, a giggle or sigh,
Oh, look! A lost rubber duck just went by!

In this zany dance, our worries unwind,
A parade of odd socks, of all shapes and kind.
From kittens to cupcakes, it's all in the mix,
Frogs wearing bowties, oh look at the tricks!

Life spirals around, like roller coasters high,
With loops and wild screams, we touch the blue sky.
Laughter, our soundtrack, as we spin and sway,
Finding joy in the moments, come what may!

So, let's twirl together, in this grand music hall,
The spiral of life, oh what a ball!

Illuminated Footsteps

With twinkling sandals, we dance through the night,
Our shoes glow in colors that are out of sight.
Each step a bright sparkle, a giggle, hooray!
Follow the glowing, come join in the play!

We skip over puddles, like fish with a wink,
And chase after fireflies, oh what do you think?
The moon in a tutu, doing jazz hands so grand,
While stars join the chorus, it's a rockin' band!

As we wander these paths, with joy as our guide,
With magical footsteps, oh what a ride!
An adventure in ruffles, no worry or care,
Illuminated footprints, we'll always share!

So join in the shimmer, let's make some more noise,
In this twinkling night dance, for girls and for boys!

A Symphony of Seasons

In spring, we skip with daffodils bright,
While jumping on clouds, feeling just right.
Summer brings ice cream, in flavors galore,
As we giggle through rainstorms, and seek out a shore!

Autumn's a concert with leaves all around,
We rustle and tumble, what fun can be found!
With pumpkins that giggle and scarecrows that sway,
We dance with the breeze, just playing all day!

Winter's a party with snowflakes that spin,
Snowball fights waiting, let the fun begin!
We build snowy castles with marshmallow tops,
As laughter and cocoa make warm, cozy stops!

Together we sing in this year's crazy show,
A symphony of seasons, let the joy overflow!

Radiant Spring

In April, flowers bloom and sway,
They laugh and giggle through the day.
A bee buzzes by with a funny tune,
Sipping nectar beneath the moon.

Bunnies bounce, they leap and hop,
Chasing tails, they never stop.
A frog croaks jokes from a nearby bog,
While turtles race—like a slow-traveling fog.

The sun shines bright, a joker's grin,
Tickling grass, making it spin.
Kids in mud, with laughter loud,
Creating masterpieces, proud and unbowed.

As springtime unfolds, chaos prevails,
Squirrels plot heists for shiny tales.
Nature's circus, merry and mad,
Just look at the antics—oh, how it's rad!

The Wind's Gentle Embrace

The wind whispers jokes among the trees,
Tickling branches, dancing with ease.
A leaf spins round, a dizzy delight,
Telling the flowers to hold on tight.

Clouds in the sky play hide and seek,
With sunlight peeking, so cheeky and sleek.
A kite is tangled with an old bird's nest,
As the breeze laughs hard at our silly quest.

Dandelions declare a fierce balloon war,
Puffing seeds out, oh, what a score!
Children run laughing, arms out wide,
While the wind's playful humor takes us for a ride.

Nature's comedy show, never a bore,
With each gust, there's always more.
So when you hear the breeze softly tease,
Join in the laughter—it's sure to please!

Constellations of Change

Stars twinkle brightly, like winking eyes,
Each one holding the funniest of ties.
A comet zooms by with a giggly grace,
And moonbeams chuckle as they light up space.

Planets argue, with high-pitched voices,
About who's brightest—making bold choices.
The Milky Way spills popcorn from its milky way,
As asteroids tumble in a comedic ballet.

Black holes joke, 'We just suck all the fun!'
While supernovae burst, making wishes run.
Galaxies swirl in a cosmic dance,
Encouraging stardust to take a chance.

So when you look up with a curious eye,
Remember the humor that fills the sky.
In this universe, we're all part of the show,
Embracing the magic as we twinkle and glow!

A Dance of Leaves

Leaves pirouette, spinning with flair,
Whispering secrets in the crisp autumn air.
A gust of wind plays tag through the trees,
While acorns giggle, 'Just watch us tease!'

The maples wear jackets of red and gold,
As if bragging about stories bold.
A squirrel chortles, tending his stash,
While dancing down branches in a mad dash.

Pumpkins roll in with a funny frown,
Where smiles abound in a playful town.
Children jump into piles with glee,
Kicking up leaves—oh, come join me!

So twirl and tumble in nature's play,
Find joy in the little things every day.
In the rustling leaves, let laughter be found,
For in this dance, silliness abounds!

Under the Canopy of Dreams

Under trees of ticklish leaves,
We dance with squirrels, oh what a tease!
Branches giggle, swaying so light,
While we trip over roots in delight.

In the shade, we share silly tales,
Of flying fish and singing snails.
A picnic spread with jam on pants,
As the ants join in the goofy dance.

Each freckled sunbeam beams with glee,
Whispering secrets just for me.
We bounce on clouds like cotton candy,
In this world, everything feels dandy.

With dreams as bright as mismatched socks,
We giggle loud, we love to box.
Under the canopy, laughter grows,
Life's a joke, and oh how it flows!

Blossoming Beyond Borders

Petals painted in funky hues,
Dancing to the silliest news.
A flower sings about lost socks,
While bees join in with tiny talks.

Blossoms stretch in a wild parade,
Chasing butterflies with silly charades.
Sunshine and giggles, what a sight,
In a garden where all feels right.

Each plant loves to poke and prod,
Pointing out the dancing clod.
"Look at us!" the daisies shout,
As the tulips join in the clout.

Beyond the fence, the world is bright,
All we need is laughter's light.
In this patch, we play, we tease,
Nature's jest, a joyful breeze!

Emerging from Silence

In the hush of the early morn,
Comes a giggle, sweetly born.
A snail slides in with a comic frown,
Bouncing along - the best in town!

From shadows, whispers begin to play,
As sleepy critters awake in ballet.
A mouse wears slippers, what a sight!
Oh what fun in the morning light!

Even the rocks begin to sing,
With each note, they start to swing.
A dance party in the quiet glade,
Where every critter is unafraid!

Emerging from silence, laughter roars,
It's a comedy show behind closed doors.
With nature's quirks, we all unite,
Embracing the silliness, pure delight!

The Art of Becoming

With clay in hand, we shape our dreams,
Laughter bubbles like cool streams.
A pot that looks more like a frog,
Turns into art in a joyful fog.

Each mistake is a masterpiece,
A wonky vase brings so much peace.
Fingers slip, some colors clash,
In the end, it's worth the splash!

From giggles to grins, we craft our way,
Decorating life in bright display.
For every flop, a chuckle near,
In the mess, we find our cheer.

The art of becoming is a funny thing,
Like cat in a hat wearing a bling.
With joy we mold, and we agree,
Each silly shape sets our spirits free!

The Bloom After the Storm

Raindrops tap dance on my head,
As flowers peek from their muddy bed.
Sneaky seeds stretching on display,
Waving at clouds that fade away.

The daisies giggle, looking so proud,
While sunflowers sway like a crowd.
They whisper secrets of growth and cheer,
"Watch us shine, the moody sky's clear!"

Each petal's laugh is a wild delight,
As they jive in the warm daylight.
With roots in soil, they know what's real,
This nature's jest is quite the deal.

A storm can't stop their whimsy spree,
They bloom with glee in jubilee.
Oh to be a flower, no worries, just ease,
Dancing through puddles like a breeze!

Where Courage Meets the Soil

Underneath the dirt, dreams coalesce,
Tiny sprouts preparing for their quest.
With wiggles and chuckles, they start to wake,
Bold little leaves, ready to stake.

Worms offer advice, wise and spry,
"Stick to your roots, don't be shy!"
The sun gives a wink, the rain nods too,
Encouraging the green, amidst the dew.

Bugs pop in with a laugh and grin,
"You, brave little plant, let the fun begin!"
They throw a party, a garden delight,
With roots tapping songs, all through the night.

Courage is sprouting in soil so deep,
With every wiggle, no secret to keep.
In this patch of laughter, foliage grows,
It's a jolly fest where everyone knows!

Tracing Horizons of Change

Once a little seed, sleepy and small,
Dreamed of adventure beyond the fall.
It rolled and tumbled, oh what a scene,
Chasing sunsets, bright and serene.

Stretching its limbs to feel the breeze,
Finding its way through playful trees.
With every twist, it giggles and spins,
Creating stories where the fun begins.

The skies burst with colors, a joyful affair,
As clouds cheer on this floating dare.
Tiny hands of sun and rain unite,
Whirling the seed through the calm twilight.

Tracing horizons, the seed cries out,
"Life's a funny game, there's never a doubt!"
With every change, it dances in light,
In the grand old garden of day and night.

The Gentle Rise

From the ground up, a tale unfolds,
With roots that dance, and laughter that holds.
Tiny shoots peek, filled with delight,
Like cheerleaders in a green, sunny light.

As they stretch upwards, they play and tease,
Tickling the squirrels hanging in trees.
A gentle rise, oh such a fun sight,
They giggle along, full of sheer delight.

The breeze says, "Come play, let's have some fun!"
While daisies and dandelions race, everyone!
With petals waving like flags on parade,
They celebrate the gifts that a garden has made.

In the gentle rise, joy fills the air,
With hilarity blooming everywhere.
Seeds of mischief, spun in a twirl,
Growing together in this whimsical world!

Transcending Limits

I tried to climb a tree one day,
But squirrels laughed and called me 'sway.'
I reached for fruit but grabbed a shoe,
Now I'm the meme, thanks to my crew.

Why not just fly or leap so high?
My dreams took off, but I didn't fly!
I tripped on a root, did a wild spin,
Guess gravity wins; let's try again.

I donned a cape, pretended to soar,
But realized my dreams hit the floor.
A gust of wind knocked me right down,
Now I'm the hero of 'clumsy town!'

With laughter echoing through the trees,
I'll stick to ground and maybe cheese.
Life's funny bends, oh what a blast,
In this comedy, I'm unsurpassed!

Nature's Secret Lessons

The flowers danced in silly cheer,
While bees wore tiny hats, oh dear!
A sunflower winked, then said with glee,
'You can't wear shoes; just be a bee!'

The trees all giggled, swayed to the left,
While branches shared tales of summer's theft.
'What's the secret?' I asked in jest,
They whispered, 'Just laugh, it's really the best!'

A squirrel dropped a nut with flair,
Right on my head, it seemed quite rare.
"I'm teaching you wisdom," he chattered bright,
"Life's better shared with a friendly bite!"

From petals to nuts, the wisdom abounds,
In nature's laugh, joy truly resounds.
So take a stroll, let silliness flow,
In every moment, there's magic to grow!

Wings of Aspiration

I built a pair of wings from leaves,
To fly like birds, oh the webs it weaves!
But up I went and down I fell,
Now I'm stuck in a tall tree shell.

Friends laughed hard as I tried to soar,
With duct tape wings as I hit the floor.
'I'm an eagle!' I cried, but couldn't take flight,
More like a pigeon 'round dinner tonight.

Chasing dreams can be quite a trip,
Like aiming to cook when you can't even whip.
But dreams are fine; with a grin on my face,
I'll launch again, at my own silly pace!

So here's to jest, and flights of the mind,
With laughter as fuel, true joy you'll find.
While wings may not work, I'll dance in the breeze,
In this world of whimsy, I'm sure to tease!

Echoes of the Past

I found an old shoe beneath my bed,
Wondered if it still fits my silly head!
The ghosts of my youth whispered so clear,
'If it doesn't fit, just try not to cheer!'

I dug through the attic, what a wild sight,
Old toys and games, oh what delight!
A comb from the '80s, a beeper too,
Each relic laughed, bursting with hue.

I clutched a diary covered in dust,
Read my crushes, my dreams, and vast gusts.
'Imagine if I'd text them today,
With all those emojis, what would they say?'

So echoes resound and memories blend,
In jest, I recall days that won't end.
I'll laugh with the shadows, dance with the past,
In a world so quirky, I'll have a blast!

Whispers of Flourishing

In the garden, plants have flair,
They gossip softly in the air.
"I don't sprout, just want some sun,
Why does the weeder think it's fun?"

Tiny seeds plot through the night,
Dream of growing tall and bright.
"I'll outshine that dandelion,
With my bloom, what a fashion!"

Every bud a secret told,
Hiding jokes as they unfold.
"Be careful, don't spill your beans,
Or we'll be stuck in veggie scenes!"

So here's to blooms that tease and play,
In this jungle, make my day!
Laughter sprouts with each new sprig,
Finding humor in the big!

Embracing the Unfolding

A cactus wore a party hat,
Said, "Why nutmeg? I'm no cat!"
While daisies danced in the breeze,
Wiggling roots just to tease.

Leaves whisper soft secrets too,
"Did you hear? The soil's new!"
Tulips giggle, swaying low,
Tripping over worms, oh no!

Sunflower stood, a tall, proud sight,
Told jokes that gave us a fright.
"Why did the rose date a thorn?
To feel sharp, and a bit worn!"

So here's to buds and blooms so bright,
Filling the garden with delight.
In every twist and every bend,
Life's puns are sure to recommend!

The Dance of Yearning Roots

Roots are waltzing down below,
Shaking off the dirt and woe.
"I wish my stem would stretch a bit,
And dance like me without a split!"

Little shoots peek through the ground,
Sass and jokes in every sound.
"Why do plants always need a drink?
To hear their leaves laugh and think!"

A flower tried to do the splits,
Fell right down — oh, what a hit!
"I only wanted to impress,
But now I'm lying in this mess!"

Yet in the soil, there's no shame,
We're all just growing in this game.
A twist, a turn, a funny spout,
Nature's humor—check it out!

Seasons of Becoming

In spring, the leaves hold a debate,
"Which of us will soon feel great?"
"I think it's me, I've got the flair,
Just check out all my vibrant hair!"

Summer blooms with bright, sunny glee,
"Hey, cool down! Don't envy me!"
As sunbeams tease the timid buds,
"Dance with joy or face the floods!"

In fall, leaves crack jokes on the floor,
"We're not dead—we're just out the door!"
Orange and yellow, their funny hats,
Who knew they could ditch the spats?

Winter whispers from afar,
"I've got snowflakes, who needs a car?"
Each season chimes with laughter clear,
In the dance of life, bring good cheer!

Woven with the Threads of Time

In the fabric of a Monday, I found my old sock,
It matched my left foot, but on the right it did dock.
Stitched with laughter from moments quite silly,
I'll wear it with pride, though the neighbors may thrill-y.

The clock ticked backward, what a sight to behold,
Time takes funny twists, like a jester so bold.
In the dance of a Tuesday, I tripped with a child,
We both tumbled down, but each giggle beguiled.

Thursdays sprout wisdom, like weeds in a patch,
I pull out my book, it's not really a match.
Stories of heroes, but they all seem to flail,
As their plans unravel like a comedic tale.

With Fridays now looming, my pet cat gives chase,
He zarred through the room in a whirlwind of grace.
Knock knock, who's there? Oh, it's just a good laugh,
Time's woven our paths in a colorful half.

Tending the Heart's Garden

In a garden of giggles, where daisies poke fun,
I planted my hopes with a sprinkle of sun.
Watering laughter while weeds sprouted clowns,
Every joke was a petal, the giggles were crowns.

The bees buzzed with puns, such a sweet little tune,
While butterflies fluttered in conga lines soon.
But a gopher came up, oh must've been blind,
He dug up my daisies, left tulips behind.

I chatted with worms, they had wisdom to share,
"Don't fret over losses; just grow some more hair!"
They wriggled with mirth in a composted bed,
"Compost your troubles, and eat cake instead!"

With each seed sown, the blossoms of joy,
Turned grumbles to giggles in festival ploy.
Tending to what's funny, my heart learned to sing,
In this garden of laughter, I feel like a king!

The Alchemy of Change

In a cauldron of chaos, I mixed up a brew,
My potion of pancakes turned out to be glue.
I stirred up my socks and a rhubarb or two,
The alchemy's funny, with magic askew.

With a pinch of giggles and a dash of regret,
I turned my goldfish into a pet trumpet,
It blew bubbles of laughter, and man, what a sight,
As the cat joined the band, keeping rhythm just right.

Turnips transformed into squawking old hats,
While owls began spinning webbed dances with bats.
With each little change, the world turned around,
And the stage of my life became comedy ground.

As I waved my odd wand, the crowd gave a cheer,
"More magic!" they shouted, "Let's drink up some beer!"

The alchemy's golden, with laughter the key,
Transforming the mundane into glee so carefree!

Fostering the Infinite

In a room full of echoes, I fostered a laugh,
It grew like a giant from a small little gaffe.
I tickled a pickle, who offered a dance,
Now pickles on roller skates have got quite a chance!

The infinite giggles stretched wide like the sea,
With bubbles of joy that just danced to be free.
A squirrel with a monocle narrated the tale,
Of snickers and chuckles that left us all frail.

I captured a smile and sent it to space,
Where astronauts sported my very own grace.
With humor as fuel, they zoomed around Mars,
The galaxies giggle, swappin' laughter in jars.

So, let's foster these moments, each one a delight,
For in laughter's vastness, we find purest light.
With friends, pets, and pickles, we'll sparkle and shine,
Creating infinity, one chuckle at a time!

Embracing the Unknown

I stepped outside, shoes on the wrong feet,
My neighbor laughed, oh what a treat!
With every twist that my path may take,
I trip on life, but make no mistake.

The sky is gray, my hat's on too tight,
I dance like a chicken, what a weird sight!
In the middle of chaos, I find my groove,
Laughing at worries, I'm starting to move.

Lost my train of thought, it's on another track,
Chasing lost socks, it's a full-time knack!
With every stumble, I stand up and grin,
Embracing the odd, let the fun begin!

So here's to the wild, the wacky, the strange,
Life's a big circus, always in range.
With giggles and gaffes, we dance and we play,
Making the most of this zany ballet.

A Tapestry of Hope

Thread by thread, I stitch with flair,
My cat on the table, causing despair.
Each knot, a laugh, each color, a dream,
Weave in the quirks, let life be supreme!

From tangled yarns, I pull out a braid,
The dog is now tangled, but what's there to trade?
With each silly snip, creativity flows,
Like candy in jars, here's how life glows.

A splash of blue, a dash of red,
My coffee's cold, but I'll sip instead.
With scissors and puns, I create and inspire,
Crafting a world that's filled with desire.

Each poke and a prod, a giggle or two,
As I stitch through the mess, it all feels brand new.
In the fabric of life, I find my delight,
Dancing through chaos, my canvas feels bright.

The Soil of Possibility

In a garden of giggles, I scatter my seeds,
Wondering just what each sprout really needs.
Water's a laugh, sunbeams a cheer,
Digging through dirt, I shed silly fear.

With worms doing tango, they twist and they twirl,
Each turn of the shovel gives dreams a whirl.
I talk to the daisies, they nod and they sway,
While carrots wear shades, they brighten my day.

A sprinkle of joy as I weed out the frowns,
The gnomes in my patch wear the silliest gowns.
A harvest of giggles, that's all that I sow,
Life's messy and funny, just let it all flow.

So join in the fun, plant seeds of delight,
In the soil of our hearts, we'll grow it just right.
With laughter as sunlight, and joy as the rain,
We'll cultivate dreams, time and time again!

The Song of the Unseen

Listen, oh listener, to giggles in the wind,
A tune plays softly, where chaos has sinned.
The birds have their banter, the squirrels join in,
In this symphony silly, where do we begin?

With whispers of mischief, the breeze makes me chuckle,

As leaves dance around, in a whimsical shuffle.
The trees sway along, with laughter so deep,
A melody's formed, it's a song we all keep.

The shadows of jokes flicker under the sun,
Each chuckle a note, in this harmony spun.
Let's prance like the clouds, with no care or plight,
As the world hums a tune, embracing the light.

In this orchestra wild, we join hand in hand,
All silly and merry, let's take a stand.
For the song never ends, it just plays on repeat,
In the laughter of life, we all find our beat.

Midnight Blossoms

In the quiet of night, blooms start to dance,
Unruly petals twirl, as if by chance.
They giggle with glee, do their little show,
Under the moonlight, putting on a glow.

With fireflies as partners, they sway around,
The oddest flower mixes, it's quite profound.
Who knew they could boogie when no one is near?
Midnight's bouquet, let's all give a cheer!

They tell silly jokes about the morning dew,
Claiming they've outshone the sun, it's true!
But these are just whispers among the leaves,
In the garden of dreams where laughter weaves.

So next time you wander, don't rush by fast,
Stop a while, laugh, make memories last.
For in every giggle, a secret is found,
In the night's soft embrace, we all spin around.

The Warmth of New Beginnings

A sprout peeks out, in a race to the sky,
Waving at clouds, as they drift by.
With sunshine and giggles, it sprouts quite proud,
"Watch out world, I'm not shy!" it shouts loud.

The birds sing along, toss seeds without care,
Creating a ruckus, a whimsical air.
"I'm just a wee seed, but watch me go far!"
Says the tiny green shoot, "I'll reach for a star!"

But what's this? A bunny hops in to play,
Nibbles the leaves, "Oh dear, not today!"
The sprout shakes its head, with a playful grin,
"Just wait 'til I bloom, then I'll take you in!"

So, dance little sprout, in the warmth of the sun,
Learning to grow while having some fun.
In every new start, giggles take flight,
In the rhythm of life, everything feels right.

Harvesting Wisdom

Old trees share secrets with the rustling breeze,
"Have a good laugh, and sprout from the knees!"
They chuckle and crack, like an old wooden chair,
Reminding young shoots, that laughter's the fare.

In the orchard of thoughts, apples drop low,
"Pick me! I'm ripe!" says the one with a glow.
But beware of the worms, who dance in delight,
They say wisdom comes best with a pinch of a bite!

Each harvest of lessons, a basket so bright,
Filled with the joy of each silly fright.
From tripping on roots to a branch that won't shake,
The wisdom we gain is the best kind of cake.

So gather your giggles and stack them with care,
In the farm of your heart, let love be the air.
For in each little chuckle, life's treasures appear,
Sow seeds of laughter, reaping joy year after year.

Beyond the Horizon

Where mountains meet skies, and dreams start to fly,
There's a realm of laughter, like pie in the sky.
Tall grass tips its hat to the butterflies bold,
As they whisper of journeys, both new and old.

A clown-like cactus, with a great big grin,
Says, "Life's like a party; let the fun begin!"
With colorful blooms and a chuckling breeze,
Adventure awaits; just say "yes, please!"

The sun starts to giggle, painting all gold,
A canvas of happiness, a story retold.
For beyond every hill, there's more joy to find,
In the whimsy of moments, leave worries behind.

So leap like the bunnies, explore without fear,
Life's tapestry sparkles when laughter is near.
So wave at the horizon, dreams in full swing,
For the journey of joy is the best kind of fling!

Blossoms of Resilience

In the garden of my dreams, they bloom,
With silly hats and brooms,
Dancing around like they own the place,
Poking fun at time and space.

Bumblebees giggle as they buzz,
Wearing tiny boots, just because,
While daisies in dresses sway with glee,
Sparking joy like a wild spree.

From concrete cracks, they find a way,
Telling weeds, 'We're here to stay!'
Doing the tango, they wiggle and twist,
Nature's party, none can resist.

With each laugh, a shoot appears,
Filling hearts with cheer, not fears,
In this patch of wild delight,
Everything feels perfectly right.

Seeds of Gentle Change

Tiny seeds beneath the dirt,
Plotting schemes and silly flirt,
They sprout up with a cheeky grin,
Saying, 'Let the fun begin!'

They twist and twirl, a playful race,
Out of soil, they pop with grace,
Cracking jokes with every root,
In their leafy suits, so cute.

Sunshine tickles, rain comes down,
Puddle-jumping, they won't frown,
They play hopscotch on the breeze,
Showing off like they aim to please.

Through gentle nudges, they expand,
Grinning wide, they take a stand,
In every corner, laughs unfold,
Nature's story, joy retold.

The Stretching Branches of Hope

Branches stretch, and limbs sway free,
Making shadow puppets for me,
A wiggly line on the forest floor,
Silly shapes wanting more and more.

They whisper tales to passing clouds,
In their embrace, the wind loud,
Turn left, turn right, do the twist,
Frolicking roots, oh, what a list!

Swallowtails chase in a bright parade,
While squirrels juggle, never afraid,
One branch slips on a slick marshmallow,
Singing songs, oh so mellow.

In this woodland of eccentric grace,
Every leaf wears a smiley face,
With giggles echoing to each pine,
Every moment feels divine.

In the Shade of Transformation

Under trees where the giggles play,
Laughter flows like a sunlit ray,
Critters nestle in leafy beds,
Swapping stories instead of threads.

Caterpillars host a feast so grand,
Sipping dew from their fine glass stand,
With every bite, they burst with cheer,
Life's a banquet, come lend an ear!

When one leaf flutters, others shake,
Jumping in the breeze, they bake,
Cookies made of dreams and light,
Transforming dark into pure delight.

Every shade holds a secret treat,
With quirky friends, life feels so sweet,
In this grove, where laughter thrives,
Nature's magic, where joy arrives.

Harvesting Inner Light

In my garden of thoughts, weeds sprout,
Tweezers in hand, I knock them out.
Sunshine giggles, clouds play tag,
My inner glow's in a vibrant rag.

Laughter blooms amidst the dirt,
Sunflower hats—oh, what a flirt!
Mushrooms dance in the moonlight beam,
Who knew my mind was a silly team?

Overgrown hopes with tangled vines,
Pruning back dreams that dodge the signs.
While growing up might sound so grand,
Who needs a plan when fun's at hand?

So I gather light with a winky grin,
Through silly slips, I thrive within.
For every stumble, there's wit to find,
Harvesting joy, leaving doubt behind.

A Journey through the Thicket

Once I charged through brambles thick,
With a trusty stick, armed for a kick.
Why did I think I could just stroll?
Ah, the thorns had their own console!

Brush with laughter, a twist, a shout,
Lost my shoe in a merry rout.
Yet with each snag, I find a jest,
This tangled path is quite the quest.

Bumblebees buzz as they eye my snacks,
I wave hello, they give me flaks.
Who knew the buzzing could be a song,
In this wild maze where I belong?

So onward I shuffle with a snicker,
Every wrong turn makes the tale thicker.
Through the thicket, I leap and bound,
In this silly journey, fun's the crown.

The Heart's Quiet Expansion

My heart's a balloon filled with cheer,
Inflating slowly, year by year.
Had a pop last week, oh what a scare,
Now it's growing, with room to spare.

It dances softly, flutters about,
A giggle escapes, swirling without.
As it expands, I sip my tea,
Wondering how big it'll soon be!

Pillow fights with thoughts and schemes,
Every day bursting with new daydreams.
I paint the walls with colors bright,
In this expansion, there's pure delight.

So while it stretches, I wear a grin,
Holding my breath to let the fun in.
With every thump of my happy heart,
This quiet growth is my favorite art.

Echoes of New Beginnings

The dawn breaks with a playful laugh,
As dreams tumble like a silly giraffe.
Each echo whispers, "Try again!"
In this dance of life, I'll spin like a hen.

With every sunrise, I muse and sway,
Cracking jokes about yesterday.
Tripping over hopes isn't a sin,
With each giggle, I wear a grin.

New beginnings poke with a sneak,
You can't lose if you're funny and meek.
So let's fumble forth with hearts aglow,
In this circus of life, let the laughter flow.

For each fresh start is a chance to play,
To trip and tumble in a goofy way.
In echoes of joy, I'll make my stand,
Finding magic in the chaos at hand.

Lanterns in the Garden

In the garden, lights appear,
Glowworms thinking they are dear.
They wiggle and dance in pure delight,
Stealing the show, oh what a sight!

A beetle dressed in fancy hat,
Says, "Why's the rabbit such a brat?"
He hops around, so full of glee,
While ants all laugh, 'It's just a spree!'

The gnomes whisper secrets of the night,
About a frog who dreams of flight.
With wings made of leaves, he takes a leap,
And croaks, "I'm ready, let's not sleep!"

In this garden, nothing stays still,
Each character brings a new thrill.
With laughter bright, the moon does glow,
In our antics, we steal the show!

Veins of Strength

Roots like spaghetti, tangled and thick,
Fumbling their way, oh what a trick!
They whisper tales of days gone by,
While saplings giggle, reaching the sky.

A wise old oak in his Sunday best,
Boasts of storms he's faced, never stressed.
"Try a little rain, it's not a crime,
I'll sip my tea, it's quite sublime!"

The tulips gossip, in colors so bright,
"Who wore it best? The daisy or knight?"
But just then a squirrel, full of flair,
Screeches, "Fashion here is so rare!"

In this kingdom of green and glee,
Strength is measured in a cup of tea.
With fortitude wrapped in laughter's jest,
We find our joy, it's truly the best!

The Silent Symphony of Growth

In the hush of dawn, seeds take a bow,
With whispered hopes, they're ready now.
Each tiny sprout with dreams to sell,
Plays the tune of life so well.

A ladybug conducts the show,
Tapping rhythm, "Let's go, let's grow!"
The daisies sway, a floral choir,
As sunlight beams, lifting them higher.

A worm in the back, he steals the scene,
Does the worm dance, oh so keen!
He wiggles and giggles, what a sight,
In this silent show, everything's right.

As soil sings low, and roots hum along,
Life's a melody, sweet and strong.
In every bloom, a story's unfurled,
Together we march, it's our weird world!

Embracing Change's Embrace

The caterpillar sat, feeling so shy,
"Why do I have to grow wings, oh my?"
But the butterflies laughed, "Don't you fret,
Transformation is fun, you'll be all set!"

With a wink and a nudge, he took a leap,
Into a cocoon, oh so deep!
Days passed by with dreams and spins,
Then out he came, with sparkly fins!

A frog by the pond gives a ribbit of cheer,
"Embrace the change, come swim over here!"
With splashes of joy, they hop and glide,
In the dance of life, let laughter reside.

So here's to the wiggles, the jigs, and jiggles,
Life's not a maze of straight lines and giggles.
In every twist, let smiles embrace,
For fun in the journey is truly the grace!

www.ingramcontent.com/pod-product-compliance
Lightning Source LLC
Chambersburg PA
CBHW070750220426
43209CB00083B/235